MAKING IT WORK

Stephen Gaukroger

Scripture Union
130 City Road, London EC1V 2NJ

© 1989 Stephen Gaukroger.
First published March 1989 by Scripture Union,
130 City Road, London EC1V 2NJ

ISBN 0 86201 506 5

British Library Cataloguing in Publication Data

Gaukroger, Stephen, *1954–*
    Making it Work
    1. Christian life
    I. Title
    248.4

    ISBN 0–86201–506–5

Illustrations: Simon Jenkins

Phototypeset by Input Typesetting Ltd, London.
Printed and bound in Great Britain by Cox & Wyman
Ltd, Reading.

Contents

Thanks to . .

My parents, for laying such
good foundations in my own
life.

Stopsley Baptist Church, for
their continuing love and
support.

Brenda and Becky, for their
hard work and constant
encouragement.

JLM, BJ and CE, whom I love.

1
Starting Out

So you've become a Christian. Congratulations! It's the most important commitment you could ever have made.

The potential for every new Christian is incredible; so much so that, at the moment, you only have the merest glimmer of what could be in store for you. Every wrong thing you have done has been forgiven. You have become a new person, a child of God with an incredible heavenly Father. For you, death is not the end of everything because you have been given God's cast-iron guarantee of life with him for ever. Your eternal future is absolutely secure. There are so many other things to take advantage of too – a new family to love and support you, a special power in your life to defeat wrong and to help others, different kinds of gifts God wants you to have . . . the list could go on and on.

It sounds too good to be true, but it is not! Sadly, many Christians do not experience all these things

Page 999

... and then there's the fact that God loves you even when you go wrong, and

P.T.O.

in the way God wants them to. But they are available, even if some Christians do not take advantage of them.

This book lays the foundations for living a strong Christian life and points to some of its possibilities. You are at the beginning of a long climb. It will often be difficult, you will sometimes feel like giving up, and there will be times when you feel that you are making no progress at all. Thankfully, you will be encouraged along the way; the clouds will lift and the scenery will be breathtaking. In these moments you will know you are on the right track and the view will spur you on to greater heights. Throughout your life you will continue the climb and at the summit you will discover a new view too marvellous to be described in words!

You may be reeling from the excitement of all this or wondering why you do not feel any different

from the way you did before your decision to become a Christian. You may be on cloud nine or underneath cloud one! Whatever your *feelings* you need to establish the *facts* about what has happened to you.

And facts they most certainly are. It is a fact of history that Jesus lived and died. That he was raised from the dead is supported by substantial evidence and no one has been able to disprove it, despite numerous attempts to do so. All the facts are recorded in a Bible which, contrary to popular opinion, is not riddled with contradictions or errors. It is a thoroughly reliable, well-attested document. Even in the face of challenges from scientists, politicians and philosophers, the Christian faith emerges with clear, sensible answers.

So what have you done in becoming a Christian? You have joined millions of others in a faith based on fact. These facts show that God has made the human race a marvellous offer. He knows the mess we are in and he wants us to discover his solution. We need to be genuinely sorry for the wrong we have done and ready to turn our back on our old way of life. This is what it means to *repent*. After this, we must trust that through the death of Jesus, God will forgive us. This is what it means to *have faith*. When these two things happen God comes to make his home in our lives. We become Christians.

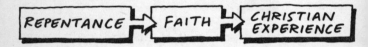

REPENTANCE → FAITH → CHRISTIAN EXPERIENCE

These early steps are vitally important. If we blow it at this stage it will be more difficult to get things together later on. It is not unusual, for example, for young children to have teeth which grow crooked. A brace can correct this fairly quickly, but if they are left to continue growing crooked into adulthood the same problem may take years to straighten out. So let's get our teeth into these two important subjects!

REPENTANCE

This means more than just being sorry. Many a criminal has stood in court telling a judge he was sorry. He might simply mean, 'I'm sorry I got caught'! If he commits the same crime a week after being released we are probably not going to believe that his courtroom apology was sincere. Repentance is the opposite of this. It does mean being sorry, but it also means *being sorry enough to change*; to turn our backs on our own way and want to go God's way; an about-face, a U-turn, a 180° change of direction. Billy Graham puts it like this,

'If your sorrow is because certain consequences have come on your family because of your sin, this is remorse, not true repentance. If on the other hand, you are grieved because you also sinned against God and his holy laws, then you are on the right road.'

Many people have fallen at this first hurdle. Some 'prayed to receive Christ' at an evangelistic meeting because they were moved by the emotion of it all. Some thought they would try Christianity because their friends were doing it; some because it seemed the thing to be 'into' at the time. The trouble is, their Christianity is now gathering dust with the skate-board and Rubik cube – once in, now definitely out! All these people wanted Christianity on the cheap – and they got what they paid for: a shoddy, third-rate substitute for the real thing. No wonder it did not last.

Repentance is an *essential* step in becoming a Christian. It could be summarized by saying to God something like this:

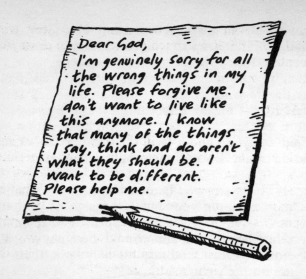

Dear God,
I'm genuinely sorry for all the wrong things in my life. Please forgive me. I don't want to live like this anymore. I know that many of the things I say, think and do aren't what they should be. I want to be different. Please help me.

God will certainly hear a prayer like this. Of course no one is pretending that a prayer of this kind is easy. It is hard enough to *say* 'sorry', never mind mean it! This kind of prayer is costly. It is painful to have to admit we have got something wrong, made a mess, failed. Anyone who enjoys saying all this must be some kind of masochist. But it is a step that cannot be avoided. To try to avoid it would be like telling the dentist that you would appreciate it if the hole in your tooth could be filled without him prodding away with any sharp instruments or using his drill. 'Sorry,' he would say, 'no drilling, no filling'! He has to get the decay out before the tooth can be repaired. If he does not you will be back in his chair within weeks, the basic problem still unresolved. Repentance is like the drilling, sometimes painful but a necessary first step to getting our lives repaired. The spiritual decay must be dealt with. When it has been dealt with God's 'filling' has a much greater chance of staying in place.

FAITH

Faith is not a blind leap in the dark. Nor is it, as a little boy once told his mother, 'believing something you know isn't true'! Faith is *belief followed by action*. If we believe that our doctor knows what he is talking about we demonstrate our belief by doing what he says – taking the medicine, avoiding certain foods or following whatever advice he may give us. To say we have faith in him and then tear up the

prescription he gives us is hypocrisy. So when we *say* we have faith that God will forgive us if we ask him, we must mean that we are convinced he will do so and we will *act* as if we believed it. That is genuine faith. If I believe that the cup of tea my wife has just brought me will not poison me, I demonstrate that belief by drinking the tea. If I am still alive several hours later my belief has been proved correct. I believe that God will forgive me if I ask him. I demonstrate this belief by actually asking him to forgive me. Several weeks later (often several seconds later!) I discover I am alive in a new way. My belief was correct.

It is obvious from all this that the genuineness of our faith is determined by whether or not we are prepared to act on it. A prayer which we might pray to make our resolve clear would be something like this:

'God, I believe you sent Jesus to die for me so that I could be forgiven. Help me to put this belief into practice. Please come into my life and help me to really trust you, not just say I do!'

You may already have prayed prayers similar to those in this chapter. Good! If not, it might be wise to read over the last few pages again, just to be certain you are clear about faith and repentance. It may be helpful to talk it through with a more experienced Christian. The rest of the book will be of very limited help until these issues are sorted out.

2
Church

For most people, no subject is guaranteed to produce a yawn more quickly than this one. The church! It has a bad TV image and many church buildings present to the community around a picture of decay and irrelevance. Many adults in Britain today only expect to visit church for 'the three sprinklings' – once with water, once with confetti, finally with dirt! Anything more than these three occasions seems a bit fanatical. After all, why should anyone living in the twentieth century want to spend time in an old, cold building where people use eighteenth-century language to sing nineteenth-century songs?

MISUNDERSTANDINGS

There are a few misunderstandings to clear up before we go on. Firstly, the picture of church life we have described is true only of *some* churches. There are *thousands* of churches in Britain today which are nothing like this. Their worship is lively and the sermons have something to say about life in the 1990s. The services are filled with vitality and energy and the people are as 'normal' as you or I. Secondly, clergymen are not all old, slightly eccentric or effeminate, despite what you may have seen on TV! Many church leaders are young and action orientated.

There is one other area which probably needs clearing up. It is this: we cannot just *go* to church, we *are* it! The Bible compares being a Christian to being part of a body. When we become Christians we become fingers or elbows or noses! In other words, when God comes into our life we become attached to other people. The thought of a thumb trying to work while cut off from the rest of the body is either funny or sick; in reality it is just not possible! Now that you have this new faith it is absolutely essential that you get thoroughly involved in a local church. Your survival as a Christian may well depend on it. Without the church you are like a soldier trying to fight a battle without a unit or a cricketer trying to play the game without a team. These are both group activities and so is the Christian life.

Years ago, a church leader was visiting a man who had become a Christian but who had decided he did not need to be part of a local church. The

leader took a live coal from the roaring fire by which they were sitting and placed it in the hearth. As their conversation continued the once blazing piece of coal began to smoulder and finally stopped burning altogether. The point was clear. However strong your new faith is, however much you 'blaze' with joy and life now, without other Christians around you your Christianity is as vulnerable and ineffective as that single piece of coal.

GETTING INVOLVED

So it is crucial to get involved with a local church. But which one? Well, you may already have one. The chances are that a friend or relative helped you to become a Christian. It usually makes sense to go to church with them. But here are some suggestions if you are confused about which church to go to.

- Do not necessarily go to the nearest church.
- Do not worry too much about which denomination it is.
- Visit several churches.
- Speak with the leaders.
- Make sure that the leaders believe the Bible is very important.
- Go to a church where you can sense God's presence in the services.

You could also try contacting the Evangelical Alliance (01-582 0228). They would be happy to advise you about a good local church

Once you are settled in a church, which you should be fairly quickly, try to understand the way it works. Who are the leaders? Who should you speak to if you have a problem or a good idea? When does it meet besides Sundays? What does this church expect of you? If you can get these things sorted out early on it will save confusion and frustration later.

This would also be a good time to raise the question of baptism. What does the church expect you to do about it? There are a number of reasons why you ought to be baptized if you have not been so already. The Bible says we should; Jesus was baptized; it is a marvellous visual aid of what God has done for us in making us clean; it is a great opportunity to demonstrate our faith publicly; it is a chance for God to touch our lives in a special way. Do not miss out on this tremendous privilege. For thousands of Christians the day of their baptism stands out as a memorable time of God's presence. Talk to the leaders about this and they will help you to prepare for your baptism and will go over the practical details with you.

FAMILY

Now that you are a Christian you have joined the family of God. Once you have got settled into your particular part of the family in Blackpool, Belfast or Basingstoke certain responsibilities and privileges will follow. Being a family member involves us in certain commitments. For example, it means we are accountable to others. No family would thrive if its members all came and went exactly when they wanted, never told anyone where they were going or why, missed meals at random, paid the bills only if they felt like it and helped around the house only when they were in the mood! Healthy family life cannot function well when its members behave like this. Neither can healthy church family life.

Aim to act responsibly from the beginning. Do

not miss things without a good reason. When you cannot be there let someone know, in advance if possible. And if you notice someone is missing ring them or perhaps call at their home. Express love and concern. Just think how bothered you would be if a member of your family failed to come home one night!

And help with the dishes! That is, don't wait around until you are asked to do an important job; if you see a need, fill it. When I was growing up my mother would come in from work and yell to us upstairs where we were playing, 'All hands on deck!' This meant everyone leapt into action to get a meal on the table. It is amazing what kind of meal can be put together in fifteen minutes when everyone joins in! 'All hands on deck!' is the cry in the church. Give out songbooks, put out chairs, deliver leaflets, give a lift to an elderly person, dig their garden, mow their lawn. Plan to be a contributing, productive church family member.

No family is perfect. Even in the happiest homes there are disagreements and tensions. The church family you join will be no exception. There will be arguments from time to time and people will say hurtful things in the heat of the moment. You may even find yourself being criticized or your motives questioned. This is *not* a cue for you to withdraw into your shell, to stop all constructive contribution or to retaliate in kind! Neither should it be an excuse to leave the church and go nowhere, or to look for another church. You do not go off and join another family because things are tough at home. No, when the going gets tough, the tough get going! Stick with it at the church, pray for the people involved, act lovingly and do not talk about it to anyone who is not in leadership.

Talking of leadership, in any family someone has to have the final say in how things are done. Church leaders have a near-impossible task and need to be helped, encouraged and obeyed by the church family. Of course, leaders are not to be followed without thought and good leaders would not want to be, but our general stance must be to get behind the leaders with our prayer and active support.

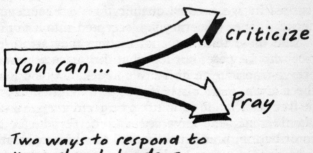

You can... criticize

Pray

Two ways to respond to your church leaders

When we have this attitude we make it easier for our leadership to guide us – and we usually need a fair bit of this sort of help as new Christians.

When you are at home you can be yourself; take your shoes off, switch on the TV, put your feet up and let your hair down – relax. In the same way, be yourself in your new church family. Forget the airs and graces and any concern for your 'image'. There is no need to pretend to be anything you are not. Family members will love us, warts and all! It is a great relief not to have to put on an act. I have known many new Christians who have found this

21

WELCOME TO
The Friendly Church
MORNING SERVICE 11.00am Sunday
EVENING SERVICE 6.30pm Sunday
PRAYER MEETING 8.00pm Tuesday

Please Wear Your Slippers!

a tremendously healing experience. For the first time in their lives they find that their worth is not judged by age, colour, qualifications or experience. Instead, they find they are accepted into a family where these things do not matter; they are loved for who they are, not for what they have achieved. Do not hesitate to enjoy this new family you have been given, particularly if your own family situation is difficult. Single people can be given a home away from home, the divorced and bereaved can be provided with another 'family' to which to relate, and children from broken homes can find security in a family which will not desert them in time of trouble!

All this brings us to the greatest privilege of being a member of the church family – we have God as our father. Read the story in the New Testament about the boy who went on a sin binge abroad and wasted his dad's hard-earned cash (Luke 15). He lost his friends, his job and his self-respect, and then had the nerve to come home. His father is no mug; the lad gets a clip round the ear and is sent off to sleep on a park bench somewhere. Well, he would have been if you or I had been the father! What *actually* happened was that he was welcomed back as a long-lost son, given a new set of clothes and had a party thrown for him!

Every Christian has this kind of father. Before we became Christians, when the last thing we wanted in our lives was God, he loved us. Even now we make mistakes, fail, sin and often get things wrong. Despite all this, our father longs for us to come back to him and waits with open arms. You have joined a family where the father is always available, always welcoming and always wanting to

comfort you. There is no problem too big, no sin too great, no failure too awful, no pit too deep, no despair too dark, *nothing* your father is not capable of dealing with. He loves you.

It is especially important to realise this if you do not have a good 'father model' in your earthly father. Perhaps he died while you were young or deserted your mother and you. Perhaps he mistreated you or seemed distant and uninterested in your life. If this is the case, do not impose onto God the feelings you associate with that idea of father. God is all that is *best* in fatherhood, magnified a thousand times over! In a supernatural way he can become the supportive father you may never have had.

3
Getting the most out of church

Many things in church life will seem strange at first but, given a little time and the patience to see how it all works, you will soon be reaping great benefits from your times with God's people. Here are some practical suggestions to help you get the most out of your local fellowship.

THE CHURCH EXPERIENCE

For a start there is no need to get dressed up in what used to be called 'Sunday best'. Just wear whatever you feel comfortable in. When you get there you will not have to pay at the door, so go straight inside. Usually the seats in the circle (if there is one) and at the back of the stalls fill up first. This means the later you are, the nearer the front you will have to sit!

Before and after the service, be ready for either of two reactions from other people: (a) lots of people speak to you; you get several invitations to lunch, and someone hugs you and says 'bless you' when you have not even sneezed! You feel completely overwhelmed by their warmth. Or (b) no one even smiles at you; they are all involved in their own conversations. No invitations home for coffee, just a limp handshake as you leave. You are completely underwhelmed by their coldness. Let us hope you get (c) – somewhere in between! Whatever happens, do not be put off. It will settle down after a while.

Whatever the other people are like, there is a lot you can do yourself to make sure you get the best out of this new 'church' experience. Try to get to the service at least five minutes before it starts (longer if you want to stand around chatting to people beforehand). There is nothing worse than rushing in late, out of breath and hassled. The service will be almost half over before you have settled down enough to concentrate on what is happening and you will have disturbed others by your last-minute entry as well. Use those vital five minutes to ask God to forgive you for any area of rebellion against him and pray that he will speak to you during the meeting. Pray specifically for those who are going to be preaching and leading worship.

When the service is over, stay where you are for a few moments of prayer. Thank God for speaking to you and ask him what needs to be put into practice during the week as a result of what you have learnt. Do not immediately rush into a conver-

sation about last night's TV or even the content of
next week's Bible study. Give God *time* in these
moments of quiet reflection to confirm his word to
you. There will still be opportunities to chat and
catch up on all the news after this. Those two
minutes will not make any difference to the news
but they could make a major difference to what you
take away of lasting value from the service!

During the service there will be times when your mind may begin to wander. Don't worry, this happens to everyone from time to time. It helps to remember that you are not a spectator but a participator. I know it *looks* as though you are a spectator, watching what happens at the front; but in fact, those leading in worship have the same role as a prompter in a play. They keep the worship on course, helping us not to forget why we are there. The congregation are the actors and God is the audience. Like good actors we want to send the audience away satisfied. Ask yourself,

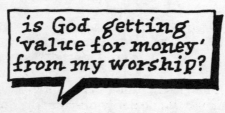

All this shows that worship is work. Try to listen to God all the time, even during announcements about the ladies' outing to Bognor and an evangelistic coffee morning; while putting money in the offering; when finding the songs, holding a Bible in one hand and a song book in the other and raising your arms in praise! It will take all your concentration! Come to Sunday worship ready to contribute the best of your mind and will to the proceedings.

Before we go on to other aspects of the service, a word of warning. Worship is not *primarily* about our feelings. Worship is rooted in the will. Unless we learn this lesson quickly we will be at the mercy of our moods. An argument with the kids, a series of late nights or a tough time at work can cripple our worship. We must make a clear statement in the face of our emotions: 'It is right to worship God. He is Lord, whether I happen to feel like it or not. He is worthy of my worship even though worshipping him is the last thing in the world I want to do. Because it is right, I am going to do it.' Now this is more easily said than done but it becomes easier the more we exercise control over our emotions and resolve to throw ourselves wholeheartedly into worship. Do not be put off by people who claim that it is hypocritical to tell God you love him when you do not feel you love anybody! My three-year-old daughter can be stubborn and wilfully disobedient; sometimes she makes me very angry. At times like this I do not like her very much at all but I still love her tremendously . . . and I tell her so! I am not being a hypocrite, I am stating a truth momentarily obscured by emotions. When my anger subsides I *feel* like loving her as well as *actually* loving her. Interestingly, the same often happens in worship. If we worship despite the way we feel we often find that our feelings come into line with the facts, and we start to feel as if we love God again. If we let our mood dictate what we do, then we end the service feeling as bad as when we started.

THE SERMON

Sitting still for twenty-five minutes (sometimes a lot longer) and listening to one person speak at you may not seem immediately appealing. It can take some getting used to. There are very few ministers who can hold you spell-bound every Sunday with their preaching: there are quite a few more who give the congregation all the thrills of watching paint dry. They couldn't preach their way out of a paper bag! Let us assume that you are listening to

someone with a genuine gift of preaching but who is still at the early stages of developing it – an average communicator. Here are some things to remember, and other things to do, in order to get the best out of the sermon.

Things to remember:
● Nobody gets it right every week. Do not criticize just because the preacher has an 'off' Sunday; pray for him.
● A lot of hard work goes into a good sermon. Do not take this for granted; thank God for the preacher's commitment.

• Your mental, emotional or physical state can affect your ability to appreciate the sermon. Do not automatically blame the speaker if you seem to get nothing from it; that might have more to do with your state of health than with the message.

• Your attitude is crucial. William Barclay had something important to say about this:

'In any church service the congregation preaches more than half the sermon. The congregation brings an atmosphere with it. That atmosphere is either a barrier through which the preacher's word cannot penetrate; or else it is such an expectancy that even the poorest sermon becomes a living flame.'

Come expectantly; you will be surprised how much the sermons improve!

Things to do:
• Bring your Bible. Follow the reading as it is read aloud and look up any references given during the sermon.

• Take notes or get a tape of the message to listen to later. You will retain much more this way and so make it easier to act on what you have heard.

• Pray during the sermon (not aloud!) asking God to show you what needs to change in your life as a result of what you are hearing.

• If there were things you did not understand, ask someone about them afterwards. Do not be too proud to confess your ignorance; if you are you will probably remain ignorant!

• If God spoke to you in a clear way during the

message, thank the speaker afterwards. Not the 'nice sermon, vicar' sort of statement; more like, 'I was really helped by what you said about . . .'

Bread and wine
In some services bread and wine are shared among the congregation. This is called Communion, the Lord's Supper or the Eucharist. You may have to stay in your seat or go to the front to receive it; you may be given your own individual glass or be asked to share an ornate chalice with others; you could be given a thin wafer of something that neither looks nor tastes like bread, or be invited to tear off a chunk of a newly-baked crusty cob.

Whatever style your own church uses, the significance of it all is the same: Jesus told Christians to do this. The bread speaks of his body and the wine of his blood. Eating the bread and drinking the wine is a reminder of the life, death and resurrection of Jesus and is an opportunity to praise him for giving us his new life. Down the centuries God has chosen to use the communion service as a time to be especially close to his people. Many Christians point back to a communion service as a time when they received healing, felt a special sense of God's presence or were given new direction in their lives. Now that you are a Christian this service is open to you. Approach it with a combination of reverence, anticipation and joy.

SMALL GROUPS

Most churches today have some kind of small group structure. Home group, house group, cell – no matter what it is called, join one! It could be the most significant factor in your spiritual growth. In one of these groups you will learn how to study the Bible, how to pray aloud, develop your spiritual gifts (see chapter 5) and maintain your sense of humour when someone disagrees with you! In a small group you can ask questions, share your own insights, ask people to pray for you and begin to pray for others. In an emergency, the house group leader is only a phone call away. Be committed to this group of people and they will be committed to you.

Do not underestimate the importance of this

activity. In the larger meetings it is very easy to remain a spectator, a critic aloof in the stands. A small group helps us to get involved with the game itself, and it is in the middle of the action that our faith is strengthened and refined. Here our weaknesses can be exposed and so corrected, and our misunderstandings about the rules can be put right as they become apparent. Being in a small group can be painful as we expose our inner selves to the gaze of others, but it is a vital part of what God wants to do in us all. Chat to one of the church leaders about this and get started in a group as soon as possible.

A natural follow-on from this is to find a 'helper' – someone to help you in your new faith. This may be someone who is in the small group and has been a Christian for a while. Ask them if they can spare you some time – an hour a week would be ideal. Use the time to read the Bible and pray together and to share things that are bothering you which you feel are too trivial or too personal to share in the group. Talk about your successes and failures in your Christian life. Ask his advice. Encourage him to be honest and to tell you if there are things that he thinks you are doing wrong. Try to accept his criticism graciously and give it careful consideration. 'Who does he think he is?!' is usually our first response, but loving correction will produce rapid spiritual growth and real Christian maturity. The help of this person will be especially valuable during your first year as a Christian. It may, of course, go on much longer than that, perhaps developing into a lifelong friendship. The aim of it is for you to grow to the point where you can pass on what you have learnt by becoming a 'helper' to someone else.

As you try to put all these things into practice, do not worry too much if you come across other bits and pieces of church life that appear confusing. Different churches have different traditions, types of service and language. If you are not sure whether to stand, sit or kneel keep half an eye on one of the 'old hands', ask the person next to you – or give up and ask someone after the service! If you think Consolations is a book in the Bible, you are not sure if Daniel is in the Old or New Testament or whether, when the plate comes round, you should put something in or take something out . . . relax! You are among friends. You really will get the hang

of it very quickly. Other people will not feel your embarrassment half as keenly as you do and before you know it you will be explaining the service, like a veteran, to someone else.

4
Enemies

When you become a Christian you change sides. From spiritual death to life, from darkness to light. Some of your old allies will notice that you have gone over to the opposition, so look out! Battle is about to commence. It will not be too long before you realize that you are in a war. I hope you were prepared a little for this before your conversion: becoming a Christian is more like joining the marines than going on a Sunday School picnic! Opposition, pressure and attack will come to every genuine believer. There will be days when you wonder why you ever joined up.

It is not all bad news though. These enemies can be identified, their tactics described and counter-measures put into effect. In this chapter we will look at the big three: the world, the flesh and the devil. Combined they form public enemy number one for the Christian.

THE WORLD

This foe takes many forms but has one purpose: to make a new Christian want to go back to the other side by robbing him or her of the benefits of the new life he or she has just received. It may take the shape of family members putting pressure on us to give up this new way of life. Many families feel extremely threatened when one of their number

'goes religious'. I have known young people be thrown out of their homes and accused of dragging the family name in the mud; husbands who have 'sent their wives to Coventry' and wives who have gone back to mother, all because of this new faith. Thankfully, nine times out of ten these separations are temporary, but they are painful. Some have been tempted to give up their new faith for the sake of peace and quiet at home. Make no mistake, family pressure can be intense.

So can pressure from friends. 'Church is OK if you like that kind of thing, but do you have to be such a fanatic?' they ask. Pressure from friends can range from gentle teasing all the way to verbal (or even physical) abuse. You may no longer find yourself 'in'; people may talk about you behind your back or avoid you altogether. In some cases you could be passed over for promotion at work or find your social life affected by a decline in popularity.

At root, this comes from the pressure to *conform*. Nothing threatens family, friends and colleagues so much as a change in you which they cannot explain. This is why they are so quick to say, 'you'll get over it once the initial excitement dies down,' and other such encouraging statements! It often gets worse as they come to understand the radical and permanent nature of the change which has taken place in you. You think about things differently, come to fresh conclusions, have new priorities and your behaviour has begun to alter. Many new Christians find themselves being overwhelmed by all this pressure to conform and find themselves drifting back into their old ways. How can we cope with this strong pull backwards?

• Find a new 'centre of security'. Most of us need people to affirm us and confirm that we are doing the right thing. In the past, family and friends have formed our place of security. Now we want to please God more than anyone else or any group of people. In practice, God delegates some of this responsibility to his people, the church. They can affirm and support us, even if all our old support systems have turned against us. Unless our centre of security shifts over to God and his people, we will always be heavily influenced by what other people think of us.

OLD CENTRE OF SECURITY

NEW CENTRE OF SECURITY

• Get help! Ask other Christians to pray for you or even come into the tough situations with you. Keep close to God and refuse to be discouraged.
• Go on the offensive! Do not just allow yourself to absorb all these blows like a spiritual punch bag. Attack! The non-Christian world loves to keep us on the defensive. They know we are in a minority and want to keep us that way. They want us to believe that we are discredited intellectually, out-dated morally and declining numerically. Do not believe a word of it! The case for Christianity has never had more compelling academic support, our moral stance is the only clear alternative to the present ethical muddle, and we are seeing a global turning to Christ which surpasses anything seen

before. So be confident about your faith. You will be surprised how quickly much of the opposition goes into retreat.

● Recognize how your conversion looks from the outside. Imagine how you would feel if someone close to you started to behave strangely. You might genuinely fear for their sanity or believe that they had been brainwashed by a weird cult. Your family and friends probably care for you a great deal. Be patient with them. Do not be arrogant or patronizing. Once they see that your new faith is genuine and that you are not going to reject them as people, things should settle down.

THE FLESH

Not only will the attack come from those around you but also from inside yourself, a kind of self-destruct mechanism. Even though your life has been given to Jesus Christ, many of the old habits, thought patterns and behaviour – 'the old me' – seem to hang around. It is as if a war is going on inside, one part wanting to go God's way, the other part the old way. Paul, one of the most famous of the early Christians, put it like this:

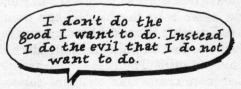

I don't do the good I want to do. Instead I do the evil that I do not want to do.

Many of us feel like this from time to time.

To win this battle with the flesh we will need to starve the old life and feed the new. It is pretty obvious that if we do this our new life will get stronger while our old life gets weaker. We do it by taking only one step at a time. If we look at everything in us which needs to be changed and attempt it all at once, we have about as much chance of success as we would trying to visit every American city in one afternoon! Conclusion: failure. Result: frustration. And not even *one* thing will get changed. Instead, we should look separately at each decision we face. Every time we decide to go God's way the new life is fed and the old starved. Each small victory makes us stronger for the next decision until, before we know it, we are dishing out some pretty lethal blows to the old life.

If we make a wrong decision it is not the end of everything. Too many new Christians think, 'Well, I've blown it. Guess I'm never going to get it right or grow strong as a Christian.' This attitude only leads on to more failure until we eventually give up. But God never gives up on us! No mistake is so drastic that he cannot forgive and correct it, if we will let him. Sometimes the flesh *will* win . . . but the God in whom we have put our trust is a God of clean sheets and fresh starts. Have you fallen over? Get up, go back to God and start again. He will honour your spiritual guts and determination.

I have often been inspired by the example of Abraham Lincoln. He should have given up long before he became President. Look at this for a catalogue of failures:

1831: Business failed
1832: Election defeat
1833: Another business failure

1834: Minor election victory
1835: Fiancée died
1836: Nervous breakdown
1838: Election defeat
1840: Election defeat
1843: Election defeat
1846: Elected to Congress
1848: Defeated in Congress election
1855: Defeated in Senate election
1856: Defeated in Vice-president election
1858: Defeated in Senate election
1860: Elected President!

Despite all this he became one of the greatest presidents America has ever had. God is not looking for people who never fail or who never get discouraged. He is looking for people with the humility to admit they have got it wrong and cannot get it right in their own strength. When they pick themselves up and look to him for his power he gladly supplies it. God is the only one with the power to defeat the flesh. All he asks for is our co-operation. Paul, whom we mentioned earlier, had to learn this lesson. In answer to his own question, 'Who will rescue me from the power of the old life?' he eventually came to this thrilling conclusion: 'Thanks to be God, who does this through our Lord Jesus Christ!'

THE DEVIL

There is so much confusion about the devil (which of course is how he likes it!) that we ought to start by saying what he is not before we look at what he is and what he does. He is *not*:

- a figment of the imagination;
- a slightly irritating, bad influence on the world who would have a pitch fork and tail if we could see him;
- an all-powerful opposing force to God.

He *is* a real, evil personality who opposes everything good. His job involves ensuring that the maximum number of people never get round to letting God sort out their lives. Should he fail with some individuals, and they do become Christians, he will be out to rob them of as much joy as possible and minimize their impact on anyone else. The Bible describes him as a cunning master of disguise with all the power of a roaring lion.

Fortunately, he is a roaring lion on a chain. God is the all-powerful keeper of the zoo and will only allow him limited freedom. Not only this, by his Son's death and resurrection God has dealt this enemy of humanity a fatal blow. So he is a mortally wounded lion on a chain! He may not be finished yet but it is only a matter of time before he is. Christians face a defeated enemy who knows his time is running out. You have nothing to fear.

However, a vicious animal in its death throes can still be very dangerous if we get too close. To treat the devil casually is to invite problems. Watch out for him particularly in two areas:

1 Stubborn habits or obsessions
These are not just things like smoking, though if you have a drug or alcohol addiction of any kind you will need to get help to deal with it immediately. Rather, is there something you simply cannot stop doing? You want to now you are a Christian, and you know you should but you just do not seem able to do anything about it. Perhaps you are a compulsive liar, addicted to pornography, an habitual gambler or consistently unreliable. Whatever the compulsion, it is an area the devil loves to exploit. He knows it is a part of your life over which God has not yet got control, and that makes it an inviting target for him. He will try to get a foothold here and begin to infect everything else from that vantage point.

2 Occult involvement
Perhaps before you became a Christian you were involved in some aspect of the occult. Maybe you

played with an ouija board, had your tarot cards read or consulted a fortune teller. You may have attempted to contact a dead relative through a medium or attended a seance. If you feel that any of these activities has a hold over you in any way, you should talk about it to someone in leadership at your church. Very little progress can be made in your spiritual life until the power of evil over your life is broken. Involvement in anything occult is an open invitation for evil forces to take up residence – they need to be made homeless as soon as possible!

If you feel the devil may be at work in you through any of these things, the three steps which follow can serve as his eviction order.

● Stop all occult involvement, even things which may appear trivial like consulting your horoscope. Destroy any books or occult paraphernalia which you have, such as the ouija board.
● Write a list of all the occult things you have done, confess them to God, repent and ask God to break the devil's influence in your life.
● Share all this with your church leaders. They may want to give time to counsel and advise you, as well as praying with you in a special way.

One final word of warning about the devil: do not keep looking for his influence in yourself or anyone else. Do not get absorbed in suspecting demons everywhere. When you discover him at work, do something about it. Otherwise get absorbed in Jesus and focus your attention on him.

5
The Holy Spirit

'With peace and love you'd think I could smile,
But when trouble comes my way I tend to run a
 mile.
And to win in this race, to keep up the pace,
I need power.'

Martyn Joseph, a Christian singer, puts his finger
on a big problem for many Christians, not just new
ones: we need power. Fortunately Jesus understands this better than we do, so he gave his
disciples a tremendous promise, 'You will receive
power when the Holy Spirit comes on you' (Acts
1:8). The Christian's power comes from God
himself, who gives his Spirit to be that power.

POWER

Too many of us try to live the Christian life by huge efforts of will: 'I must stop falling for the same old temptations.' 'I must read my Bible and pray more.' 'I must tell more of my friends about Jesus.' and so on. Of course all these things are absolutely right and we must be committed to work hard at them. *But not on our own*! When I take the family on holiday it is my responsibility to load up the car, packing the luggage into it carefully, and to strap the children in safely. It is *not* my responsibility to *push* the car all the way to the seaside! Some other source of energy (the engine) has been designed for precisely that job.

Lots of Christians are worn out and frustrated because they are pushing instead of riding. And we can begin to ride as we ask God to fill us with his Holy Spirit.

Power to serve

Boris Becker wins most of his games because he understands that the most important part of lawn tennis is the power to serve! As Christians we need to grasp that the Holy Spirit has not been given primarily to make us feel good but to equip us with power to serve.

You may be the sort of person who is enthusiastic, has lots of clever ideas, initiative, drive and boundless energy, but these are no substitute for being equipped by the Holy Spirit. God can certainly use our efforts but it is only his power which makes them effective. The Holy Spirit has given gifts to his church to help us support each other and serve the non-Christian community in which we live. You can find some of these gifts listed in 1 Corinthians 12:1-11 and Romans 12:6-8. Notice what a marvellous mixture of things are listed here. You can receive anything from the power to heal to the gift of giving your money away! The emphasis is on variety. We do not all have the same gifts but together, using our different gifts, we can encourage each other's skill in serving.

Sometimes it is obvious to see what our gifts are, but not always. If you are not sure what gifts God has given you the following steps will help you find out.

● Ask God to make clear to you what kind of gifts he has given you. Ask a friend to pray with you about it. Ask others, particularly in your house group, to tell you what kinds of gifts they see developing in you. It is often easier for *others* to see this in us than it is to see it in ourselves. Other people are usually more honest too, and help us to see what gifts we do not have!

• The leaders in your church ought to be able to provide you with some kind of 'gift discovery' questionnaire. Many Christian organizations have them and they are useful indicators of the general areas in which God may want to use you. Fill in the form and arrange an appointment with one of the leaders to discuss your findings. Do not be too hung up on the details or bound by the result for the next twenty years! These forms are helpful servants but bad masters.

• *Do something*! Attend some of the different organizations in your church. Does something stir within you when you see what they are doing? Visit that elderly couple who seem to be lonely; go with the evangelism team giving out leaflets or knocking on doors; offer a meal to a single person who is away from their close family . . . in other words, *act*. Sitting around for weeks wallowing in introspection will not help. Once we have started moving out in love to others, the areas in which God has gifted us often become clear.

Beware!

There are two opposite dangers in this area, like ravines on either side of a narrow path. The ravines are called *success* and *sadness*. To fall off on one side into 'sadness' is to view our gifts as small and insignificant, hardly missed if they were not there. Feelings of envy, and jealousy of other people's gifts characterize this ravine. To fall off on the other side into 'success' is to see our own gifts as being the major ones, believing they are indispensable to

the church and would be horribly missed if we were not there. Pride and a sense of superiority characterize this ravine.

Wise Christians walk on the path! Our gifts are different from those of other people, but equally important. We need each other's gifts to be at our most effective as a church family. They are not for competition or comparison but for co-operation. Remember this yourself and remind others if they forget . . . then perhaps none of us will fall off into the ravines!

Power to be different

All this talk about gifts for service is good but can be badly spoilt unless we are clear about the second area of the Holy Spirit's activity. He is given to make us more like Jesus. We may be filled with power in a minute and using our gifts within a month, but this part of the Holy Spirit's work goes on for a lifetime.

Being like Jesus involves becoming increasingly dominated by those qualities which characterized his life. Galatians 5:22-23 lists these qualities, describing them as the 'fruit' of the Holy Spirit. That is, these are precisely the kinds of things we should have in our lives and, as we allow the Holy Spirit to work in us, he will produce them.

And what a warm, positive set of qualities they are – love, joy, peace, patience, kindness, goodness, faithfulness, gentleness, self-control! God's plan is that we should exhibit all these things in our lives, more and more as the years go by.

So what about a bit of practical help for those committed to some serious fruit growing? Well, here are a few spiritual 'farmer's hints':

• Fruit takes time to produce. Do not be discouraged by early failure. Say sorry to God and invite the Holy Spirit to help you be more patient (or loving, etc) next time. Remember that Christianity needs the kind of approach you would take to the marathon not the hundred metres. Keep on keeping on.
• Apple trees do not produce bananas! Neither will a great deal of effort on the part of my human spirit produce the same thing as the Holy Spirit will. It

cannot. It is *his* fruit. We must be co-operating with the Spirit, allowing him more and more control of our lives. We can fake it for a while but it soon becomes too difficult to keep up the effort. It is much better to be genuinely transformed on the inside.

● Lazy farmers grow less fruit. There is no getting away from hard work in this business. Fruit trees must be nurtured, protected from birds and animals, kept free of fungus and blight and so on; no easy task. We cannot just sit back and relax while the Holy Spirit gets on with making us fruitful; that is only half the story. The other half involves the hard work of committing ourselves to getting rid of those things in our lives which hinder fruit growing. This is where a trusted Christian friend is worth their weight in gold. Ask such a

person if he or she can detect increases in your fruitfulness, or places where it might be going a bit mouldy. Pray about that person's replies and give attention to putting things right.

● Pruning is essential! Cutting out the dead wood and excess branches increases the quality and quantity of fruit. This can be painful but it is necessary if spiritual fruit is to be produced. When, for example, you ask the Holy Spirit for more of the fruit 'love', you may be in for a surprise. Instead of the warm, loving glow you are hoping to feel, God might send into your life a thoroughly objectionable character, who offends your wife and lies about you behind your back! Just when you feel like throttling him, the Lord reminds you that you asked for the love fruit to be demonstrated more in your life. This offensive person has given you the ideal opportunity to understand what true love is all about! A hurtful experience, though very difficult at the time, is often God's tool for producing a Christ-like character.

BEING FILLED WITH THE SPIRIT

At the beginning of this chapter we noted that we receive God's power for living the Christian life when we ask him to fill us with his Holy Spirit. How does this happen?

Firstly we need to understand that God *wants* to fill us with his Holy Spirit. (See Acts 1:8; Ephesians 5:18; Matthew 3:11.) He longs for us to receive all of his marvellous resources.

Then we need to take a few moments to ask God,

in a simple prayer, to fill us with himself. He will. We may feel a warm glow or a tremendous excitement. A strange language we have never learnt may come into our mind. If this happens with you, try speaking it aloud. Or we may *feel* absolutely nothing. It is important not to rely on feelings but on the fact of God's desire to fill us. We are all different and God does not impose any one, uniform experience on us. He respects our personalities.

Many people find that they receive this lovely touch from God when they are prayed for by others. Contact the leaders of your church family and ask them to arrange for someone to help you pray for the Holy Spirit's power. There might be an opportunity during one of the services to ask someone to pray with you. Do not be shy; it is great to have God bless you in a special way surrounded by his people.

Expect great things from God. He longs to flood into us with his power, so if you are prayed for and still do not seem to sense anything different, *do not give up*. If you have questions or fears, ask your church about them; share your doubts and confusions too. Occasionally God needs to heal a little damage in our lives before he can completely fill us with himself – a bit like repairing a hole in a container before filling it with water. Do not be tempted to think that you are too bad for him to fill you with himself or that God loves you less than others who seem to get 'zapped' straight away. Do not let discouragement get in the way of God pouring himself into you.

Two more things will help us continue towards

maturity in our relationship with the Holy Spirit.

Firstly, do not regard this first experience of the Holy Spirit as a once-and-for-all encounter with him. D L Moody, an American preacher in the last century, was once asked if he had been filled with the Spirit. 'Yes', he replied, 'But I leak!' He is not the only one; we all do! We need to keep asking God to fill us with himself. From time to time ask others to pray with you again for a deeper experience of the Holy Spirit. Being filled with the Holy Spirit is not the point of arrival but of departure. Too many Christians get off the train at the first station when they first realize that God is doing something in their lives. Stay on the train and you will stay on the rails!

Secondly, do not let any experiences God may give you go to your head! It is easy to look down on those who have different experiences from our own but a superior, arrogant attitude will do more than almost anything else to stop God working in us. If God gives us special experiences we should let them go to our heart not our head. We do not deserve them or earn them – they are gifts. If anything, the greater the blessing the deeper should be our humility. The more humble we are the more God can use us.

6
The Bible

Sooner or later, someone is going to mention the importance of the Bible. You will not last long (never mind grow) as a Christian without getting better acquainted with its contents.

The trouble is, getting better acquainted is a pretty daunting prospect when you first pick up a Bible, especially if the *TV Times* is the heaviest reading you usually do! But do not be put off. The New Testament has only a few more words than some of the Sunday newspapers with their colour supplements. And unlike the Sunday papers it will not be out of date on Monday – and you *can* believe what it says!

WHY READ THE BIBLE?

There are at least six very good reasons for reading the Bible:

1 God speaks through it
No other book in the world is its equal as a guide to how God thinks and what he is saying today. When you became a Christian you met the author; now read more about him in his book!

2 It tells us how to live
The Bible gives us guidelines for how to deal with almost every situation – some things to avoid and other things to do. It provides a set of values and principles to help us plot our course through the stormy waters of a world where there seems little clear sense of direction.

3 It answers our questions
What is God like? Can I be forgiven? Who is really in control of my destiny? Concerns like these are addressed in the pages of the Bible. Glenn Hoddle, England footballer and new Christian says, 'As I read the Bible I found the answers to the questions I was asking. It was like a big jigsaw puzzle, gradually falling into place.'

4 It is a spiritual antibiotic
Taken regularly the Bible provides protection against the 'disease' which attacks our Christian lives, sometimes called temptation. Without it, we are very vulnerable to the lies Satan tells us and to the pressure from others to conform to their standards.

5 It is nourishing food

Our Christian lives thrive best on a high-Bible diet. Junk-food Christians, who exist on monthly binges of celebrations and celebrity testimony stories, do not become great men and women of God. The Bible will feed our inner being and bring us assurance and strength in a way nothing else can.

6 It has power to change us

The Bible has the amazing ability to make us different. It can of course be read to inform, entertain, educate or even to savour its fine literature. But, as D L Moody pointed out, 'The Scriptures were not given to increase our knowledge, but to change our lives.' David Cohen, the General Director of Scripture Union, points out that its power to change can affect not just ourselves but our community and indeed the whole world: 'To Joshua the Lord said: "Meditate on the Book day and night so that you may be careful to do everything written in it." It would be a different world if we did.'

All this is very exciting, but you ought to know the bad news as well. (You knew there would be a catch somewhere!)

DIFFICULTIES

The Bible is not an easy book. In some places it seems impossibly complicated and in other places it appears so boring that it could be recommended as a cure for insomnia! There are several reasons for this. Firstly, it was written in a totally different period of history from our own: the most modern bits are nearly 2000 years old! It was also written in cultural and political situations vastly different from our own. Secondly, the text we read has been translated from another language, usually Greek in the New Testament and Hebrew in the Old Testament.

Thirdly, the Bible confronts the new Christian with a bewildering array of subjects, characters and types of literature. And there is more bad news to come.

The Bible is a criticized book. Many of us find that our view of the Bible has to undergo a major change when we become Christians. We used to see it as a history book with some interesting moral teaching – we may have read some of it at school.

Almost certainly we have heard that it is full of contradictions and impossible miracle stories, a jumble of ancient myths with a few profound thoughts thrown in. Suddenly, after becoming a Christian, we are asked to place our full trust in it and follow its teaching without wavering. No mean feat!

The Bible is a neglected book. It is not long before we uncover a certain hypocrisy in what is being said about the importance of the Bible. We may discover some so-called 'mature' Christians who hardly ever seem to read their Bibles and are quite ignorant about its content. We may attend church services where the Bible is read aloud briefly but hardly referred to at all afterwards. We may listen to preachers who use a Bible verse to support an idea they are trying to get across but do not seem to have much desire to discover what the Bible is actually saying! When these things happen we get the impression that the Bible is more important in theory than it is in practice.

These three items of bad news should not lead us to despair. The fact that the Bible is not easy should be seen positively rather than negatively. Anything worth having takes time and effort. Unlike the vast majority of books, we will never exhaust all that the Bible has to teach us. Scholars and ordinary Christians alike can spend decades studying it and still have more to discover. The Bible is a book great enough to keep us occupied for our whole life!

We need not be too concerned by criticisms of the Bible. The more we read it the more it convinces us of its truth. But ask hard questions about the Bible, find out as much as you can about how it came to be written and talk to a Christian leader if you discover things which appear contradictory. This is what *Time* Magazine had to say about the reliability of the Bible:

> 'After more than two centuries of facing the heaviest scientific guns that could be brought to bear, the Bible has survived – and is perhaps better for the siege. Even on the critics' own terms – historical fact – the scriptures seem more acceptable now than when the rationalists began the attack. The miraculous can be demythologized, the marvel explained, but the persistent message of the Bible will not go away.'

Similarly, do not be put off by Christians who 'talk big but live bad' when it comes to the Bible – people who stress its importance but do not live by its principles. Do not condemn them, just determine to be different. Copy the example of those who give high priority in their lives to the words of God.

GETTING INTO IT

So much for the theory, what about getting into the Bible in practice? To start with we need to have a right attitude to the Bible. As we pick it up we need to have two key thoughts at the front of our mind: reverence and humility. We do not talk much about reverence these days, even the word seems terribly dated. But if we come to the Bible casually, with a blazé or cavalier attitude, its truth will remain hidden from us. The Bible simply does not reveal its marvellous secrets to someone who approaches it like a holiday novel!

And humility. Usually we 'skim read' things until we find something that interests us – newspapers, magazines, shop catalogues, sales brochures, and so on. We assess the content as we go along. Quite the opposite happens when we read the Bible; it is assessing us! Our basic stance needs to be a willingness to obey it. Once these attitudes are in place we can tackle the practical questions about getting the most out of our Bible.

Which translation?
Try a number of different versions of the Bible to see which you feel comfortable with. I have settled on the New International Version. It is helpful to have a variety of different translations available for Bible study, but it is best to stick with just one Bible for reading in private and to take with you to church.

When is the best time to read it?
The best time to read the Bible will depend on your work schedule and family commitments. First thing in the morning might suit you best. Or lunchtimes? When the kids are in bed? Work out what is best for you and stick with it, but do not become bound by a timetable you find burdensome. Be flexible: you may have to experiment for a while to find out what is best. If you do not manage to read your Bible *every* day do not worry or feel guilty. You can still be growing as a Christian. However,

most of us find it very easy to be ill-disciplined or plain lazy about reading it, and a daily structure or plan helps us to get down to it. Sometimes it is a good idea to schedule in a prolonged period of Bible reading – say two hours to read through a whole book. You will need to plan this carefully – a couple of free hours seldom just happen!

Set aside time to read it...

Where should I start?
Not necessarily at the beginning! Try one of the Gospels, perhaps Mark. This is the shortest account of the life of Jesus. After that, one of Paul's letters or another Gospel. In the Old Testament you could work your way through Psalms and Proverbs before

tackling the history books and the prophets. All of the Bible is important but some bits are particularly helpful. Ask a Christian friend if you are not sure what to read next.

What about the difficult bits?

Use a good dictionary to look up words you do not understand. Go to a Christian bookshop and ask to see some concordances and a few commentaries. Make sure the concordance is based on the translation you are using. It will list all the words used in the Bible and tell you each verse in which it occurs. This is useful when you want to find out what the Bible says about a particular subject; it will show you where to look. Also, if you do not understand why a word is used in a particular verse, it may help to see how it is used in other verses.

Sometimes commentaries cover the whole Bible, sometimes just individual books. They help us discover the meaning of the Bible, and are especially useful when the passage we are looking at seems obscure or contains difficult concepts and ideas. One of your leaders should be able to recommend a number of helpful books in this area.

If you still cannot work out the meaning of a Bible verse or passage, ask your house group leader or some other mature Christian. They may not know the answer, but they should be able to help you to find out.

Is there any other help?

Yes, there are quite a large selection of Bible reading notes which are designed for use each day. These suggest a Bible passage to read, provide notes which pinpoint its central meaning and show different ways to apply it today. Millions of Christians use these aids and are helped tremendously by them. We should not spend more time on the notes, however, than on the Bible itself; it is the Bible that is specially inspired by God, not the writer of the notes however wonderful those notes may be! (For an idea of what books, commentaries and daily reading notes are available, see the list on page 127 headed 'To help understand the Bible.')

Using the Bible —

Read it! | Understand what it meant then... | And what it means now. | Then apply it to your life.

How can I remember what I learn?

Use a variety of approaches. Sometimes read several chapters at a sitting; on other occasions use the same length of time to meditate on a single verse or phrase. Underline or highlight bits that seem especially relevant to you, make notes in the margin if it helps fix the truth in your mind. Mull over in your mind during the day these special verses. Make an effort to memorize them too. For example, try setting yourself the target of learning one verse each week for the first year of your Christian life. Memorize a significant verse from Sunday's sermon or the housegroup Bible study. Once learnt, these verses will be there to draw on when sharing your faith with others or combating temptation.

7
Prayer

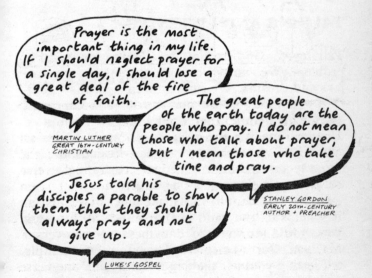

Prayer is the most important thing in my life. If I should neglect prayer for a single day, I should lose a great deal of the fire of faith.

MARTIN LUTHER
GREAT 16TH-CENTURY
CHRISTIAN

The great people of the earth today are the people who pray. I do not mean those who talk about prayer, but I mean those who take time and pray.

STANLEY GORDON
EARLY 20TH-CENTURY
AUTHOR + PREACHER

Jesus told his disciples a parable to show them that they should always pray and not give up.

LUKE'S GOSPEL

A large number of people 'say their prayers'. Relatively few learn to pray! Perhaps before you became a Christian you recited the Lord's Prayer in church, probably without thinking about it. You have almost certainly breathed a hurried prayer to God in an emergency. None of this is really prayer. Real prayer involves building a relationship with God.

This relationship-building is not easy because God cannot be touched, seen or heard through our physical senses. Most friendships develop as people talk and do things together, and that usually takes time. You cannot invite God back to your place for a coffee though, so how do you go about getting to know him?

TALKING AND LISTENING

Talking to God is not usually too much of a problem. We can tell him about our needs, pains, joys and dreams. We can thank him for his friendship and care, unload our worries and concerns, ask for his help and let him know how committed we are to making this relationship work. So far so good. But what about listening? Friendship is a two-way street and it is pretty frustrating if the traffic is only flowing in one direction.

God wants to talk to us but most of us find it hard to hear him at first. If you were in a nature reserve with the warden he might stop and say, 'Can you hear that woodpecker?' You listen carefully and hear the wind, a whole range of bird calls, an aeroplane, some strange insect sounds – everything, in fact, *except* the woodpecker! Your ear is not trained to pick out this one sound from among so many others. But the warden's is.

Our 'spiritual ears' pick up all sorts of sounds:

our own thoughts and feelings, pressure from others, religious attitudes we have grown up with, temptations from our enemy, Satan, and, among them, the voice of God. But which one *is* God's voice? With time, patience, persistence, and guidance from more experienced Christians we will develop the ability to pick out his voice. We will usually hear him most clearly when we give him our full attention. We may or may not sense that he is present. He might speak to us through the

Bible passage we are reading, through a song from the church song book, or through advice and encouragement from someone in the church fellowship. After a while he will not seem like a stranger at all.

A warning bell!

It is easy, especially for new Christians, to be fooled into thinking that we are hearing God when in fact we are only listening to ourselves. We have two main methods of checking. Firstly, we should remember that God will *never* tell us anything which goes against what he has already said in the Bible. Secondly, it is very rare to find God saying something which those in spiritual leadership believe to be wrong. It can happen, but if your church leaders do not believe that you have heard God accurately, think long and hard before you go against their advice.

Here is one very practical method of developing your listening relationship with God. You will need a Bible, a notebook, a quiet place and about twenty minutes.

● Settle your mind. Ask God to help you hear him clearly. (One minute).
● Say sorry to God for failing him and ask for his forgiveness. (Two minutes).
● Read a Bible passage slowly and several times. (Four minutes).
● Sit in quietness, asking God to help you understand what he is saying in the Bible verses. Write down any verse or idea which strikes you as particularly relevant. (Three minutes).

- Pray, asking God to make you obedient to what he has said. (Two minutes).
- Talk to God in prayer about the things which are bothering you about yourself, your friends, family, community and needs in the world. (Three minutes).
- Be quiet for a few more moments. Is there anything else God wants to say? (Two minutes).
- Thank him for his friendship. Tell him how grateful you are for all he has done for you. Sing or read a song of praise to him – it is your attitude not your voice that counts! (Three minutes).
- Invite him to spend the rest of the day with you. (One minute).

Adjust the times shown above to fit your own situation. If you find a better method use that instead, but give it time. You will find that, after a few months, you can go through this process without the mechanics of the different sections getting in the way. Add sections of your own or delete some of mine.

A COMMON MISTAKE

Many Christians do take time to read their Bible and pray, but seem to think that once they have done so they have done all that is required of them until that next 'time with God'. But no genuine relationship flourishes like this. It would be like trying to develop a friendship with no spontaneity, no dropping in for tea, no casual telephone call; insisting that you see each other only for a few

71

minutes each day (as long as something more important does not crop up!), and acting like strangers if you meet outside this structured time.

Prayer is not to be reserved only for those special times of meeting with God. It should be a characteristic of the way we live. An encouraging letter, a beautiful view, a pay-rise – thank God for them as they occur. A difficult customer, a worrying interview, a trip to the dentist – tell God your fears on the way to the appointment. Someone snubs you, someone ridicules you, someone runs into the back of your car – release your anger and hurt *to* God instead of *onto* other people! Develop 'islands of quiet' during the day, perhaps a few seconds in the

train or before you start the car, to focus back on
God. Prayer is for all day, every day; not just special
times.

PRAYING FOR A PURPOSE

All prayer has a purpose, but sometimes we or our
church family are faced with situations that require
our serious attention in prayer. It could be a major
recurring problem or a significant opportunity. The
church will have ways of responding corporately
(see below) but we can do two things personally:

1 Be persistent
Once a serious issue becomes apparent we may
sense that God is urging us to give it special attention in prayer. We can use our normal times of
prayer for this and also bring it to mind for prayer
during the day, even if just for a few moments. We
can ask other Christians we meet to pray about it
too and, if we get the opportunity, ask for special
prayer at the house group or in church on Sunday.

It is good to set aside a longer time as well to
pray just for this issue. This will probably mean
sacrificing some leisure time – but an amazing
amount of powerful praying can be done by missing
an episode of Neighbours or switching off Wogan!
If we remember to listen to God as well as talk to
him he may also give us guidance on how best to
pray. It is thrilling to see the results from this kind
of persistent praying.

George Muller, the founder of a number of
orphanages in Bristol in the nineteenth century,

emphasized the importance of being persistent in prayer:

> 'The great point is to never give up until the answer comes. I have been praying for fifty-two years, every day for two men, sons of a friend of my youth. They are not converted yet, but they will be! . . . The great fault of the children of God is, they do not continue in prayer . . . they do not persevere. If they desire anything for God's glory, they should pray until they get it.'

2 Fast

Going without food is another way to focus our minds on a specific prayer topic. The Bible tells of quite a number of occasions when God's people were encouraged to fast as a sign of how strongly they felt about an issue. Fasting adds a dimension of urgency and power to our praying.

Try it. Go without food for twenty-four hours and use for prayer the time you would normally spend eating. Simply feeling hungry will also remind you of the topic throughout the day. Do not go around telling everyone you are fasting, or putting on a pious face. It is important, however, that you explain to your husband, wife or family, well in advance, that you will not be joining them for certain meals, and why. Drink plenty of liquids and you will be fine. (If you are pregnant or have specific health problems chat first to your doctor.) You will be glad you discovered this additional aid to prayer.

PRAYING TOGETHER

Praying is like music. Instruments played on their own are good but there is a depth and richness of sound when a number play together. Praying with others will deeply enrich your own prayer life. The Bible promises God's special presence when groups meet for prayer and records some pretty spectacular answers to prayer (eg Acts 12:5-17).Get involved in praying with others. If your church has a prayer meeting, go to it. If it does not, there will be opportunities for prayer in small groups, particularly your house group. No one finds it easy to pray out loud at first, so here are some practical steps that will help you get (and give!) the most to your group's times of prayer:

● If you are really nervous, write out a brief prayer in advance, then read it during the prayer time. Or you could read out a hymn or a verse from the Bible.
● Do not pray long prayers; they can 'kill' the meeting. A good general rule is, 'Pray long in private, short in public'!

- Use ordinary language. Be real. Do not put on a pretend 'spiritual' voice. Just speak as if you were talking to a wise father.
- Pray more than once if there is time, but do not make shy people feel they have to rush to get in.
- 'One prayer, one subject' is a useful guideline. Some people mention every problem they can think of in a two-minute 'world tour'; when they say 'amen' there is nothing left for anyone else to pray about!
- Encourage other pray-ers by saying 'amen' out loud at the end of their prayers. Listen carefully to what they say so that your 'amen' can be sincere!
- Try not to 'preach' at people during your prayer or pass on juicy bits of gossip under the guise of prayer. Both of these come into the category of 'propaganda' not prayer!
- Pray positively. Avoid using prayer as an occasion for a good moan. Your positive prayer could encourage others and set a really good tone for the whole prayer time.

In many churches prayer meetings have quite a bad reputation. Even in house groups which have great social occasions and superb Bible studies, the prayer times can be as exciting as watching the test-card! Your contribution, along the lines suggested above, can make all the difference.

Prayer partners
Another excellent way to strengthen your prayer life is to find one other person with whom to pray, perhaps a member of your house group who would be committed to praying with you for half an hour

a week. Make sure you do not idle the time away with 'coffee and chat'. The regular commitment will inject discipline into your prayer life and encourage your faith as you see God answering prayer. When one partner is down, the other can encourage; when one has had a great answer to prayer, both share the joy. It is harder to slip away from following Jesus when you are involved in a 'praying duo'. The first signs of trouble are more easily detected and can be prayed about before they get out of hand.

8
Telling others

Evangelism is like *Dynasty* – you either love it or hate it! I have rarely met anyone who was neutral. Since you became a Christian you may have found that you simply cannot keep quiet about it; every conversation, whether it starts off about football or the weather, ends up with you enthusing about your new faith. If this is you, great! This chapter will give you some tools to sharpen your effectiveness still further.

If on the other hand you still feel a bit embarrassed about being a Christian or you really do not know what to say, this chapter should help get you started in telling others about this Jesus whom you have recently met.

WHY BOTHER?

Why is it so important to pass on our faith to others? There are four main reasons:

1 Gratitude and sharing

Suppose you have just made an amazing discovery – a medicine which cures cancer and heart disease within days, and has no nasty side-effects. You were critically ill but taking the medicine has brought you a complete recovery. Several of your friends have also tried it and it has had spectacular results. To keep the news of it to yourself while thousands continued to die of heart disease and cancer would be heartless and callous beyond belief. But Christians can often appear selfish in precisely this way, keeping some very good news indeed to themselves. God has forgiven the evil in our lives, erased our guilt, made us part of a new family, given us access

to a supernatural joy and peace, offered us a new power for living, guaranteed us eternal life. . . ! Gratitude compels us to let others in on the secret.

2 Obedience
Sharing our faith is not an optional extra, as if only those going for the *deluxe* version of Christianity need bother with it. When we joined God's army we recognized a new commanding officer. Our lives are now under his authority, and his wishes are clear, 'Go and make disciples of all nations', 'Go into all the world and preach the good news.' Not much room for confusion here! All Christians have a responsibility to be obedient to their Leader; every Christian soldier should play a part in recruitment.

3 God works through people
How did you become a Christian? Probably through a friend or relative. How are your family members, friends and colleagues at work going to hear the good news, if not through you? There are several helpful evangelistic techniques, but they usually depend on having formed a good relationship to begin with. The plain fact is that if people do not tell other people about Jesus then no one will find out about him!

4 Need for rescue
Men and women who reject Jesus are doomed to meaninglessness now and separation from God eternally. Only the good news we have can rescue them from their fate. If we do not provide a lifebelt we will be abandoning a drowning generation, some

of whom are going down beneath the waves of hopelessness for the third time.

HOW DO I SHARE MY FAITH?

Know your defences

As I write these words England are facing some hostile fast bowling from the West Indies in the latest test-match. English batsmen are wearing an ever more elaborate array of pads and helmets to minimize the risk of pain and injury. When faced with some of the 'bouncers' non-Christians can bowl at us, many new Christians feel as vulnerable as facing Malcolm Marshall wearing only swimming trunks!

One of the most inhibiting fears of trying to share our faith is this: will we be able to cope with the questions people throw at us? The fact is that we *can* cope a lot better than we imagine, but the way to improve our defence is to follow two principles.

Firstly, anticipate the questions. Remember all the questions that ran through your mind before you became a Christian. You know the kind of thing, 'How can Christianity be true when there are so many hypocrites in the church? Is Jesus any more than a good man? Hasn't science disproved it all anyway?' You will be pleased to know that there are only a limited number of questions which crop up, so they are fairly predictable.

Find a Christian book with some good answers to these questions and familiarize yourself with its contents. (See the titles under the heading 'Answers to questions about the Christian faith,' page 128.)

After a number of months you will feel increasingly confident at answering questions.

Occasionally, all of us get asked questions for which we do not know the answer. Just be honest and admit you do not know! No human being knows the answer to everything – and those who ask questions understand that. They are likely to be more impressed with humility and honesty than with a clever but superficial answer to every query.

Secondly, know your faith. You may not be an expert on science, other faiths, philosophy and so on but you can be an expert on your Christian faith. Compared with almost everyone at your place of work your knowledge of the Bible will soon be very good. This puts you at a real advantage. Be clear about what you believe and why. Over the years sermons and house group studies will clarify things further but it may help to read a book which will give you an overview of the Christian faith, looking at all the major themes of the Bible. (See the book suggestions on page 128 under the heading, 'Books explaining the Christian faith'.)

Go on the attack

It is not much use being well protected as a cricketer if you are just going to stand there! The aim is to score runs. Similarly, in evangelism we not only have to be able to answer people's questions but also to be ready to initiate discussion ourselves.

Attack is often the best form of defence. If someone asks us to justify our faith in the light of all the suffering in the world, we can give a reasonable answer. When we have done this we can go on the offensive and ask the questioner how *they* would explain the world's suffering. I have not heard too many good answers! Do not hesitate to turn an awkward question back to the person who asked it. Jesus used this method to great effect.

Look for openings to talk about your faith and your church family. Do not do it in a 'pious' or unnatural way, just talk about it as if you were describing a good film or chatting about something you saw on the news. As long as you do not preach at people or talk down to them, they will be interested in your activities.

Ask other people about themselves. Very few of us can resist talking about ourselves, especially with someone who is genuinely interested in us. The information you glean in this way will help form relationships and make people more open to listen to you.

Do not be afraid to appear a little 'pushy'. As long as you are gracious and polite you will be respected for standing up for your views. Remember, silence is not always golden; sometimes it is just yellow!

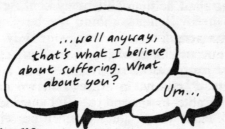

Live the life

We may have our lines of defence and attack clearly thought out, but to make them effective we need to give some attention to how our lives match up to what we say. Nothing undermines what we say about Jesus more than saying one thing and living another! Here are some hints that will help bring the two into line.

● Be relaxed. Do not become a nervous wreck by working flat out to be perfect. You are not perfect, but God will use you anyway. Besides, you will communicate your anxiety not your faith if you get too up-tight about witnessing.

- Be unflappable. Keep your cool, even when you are goaded or teased about your faith. Laughter is a great tension-reliever! Walk away rather than lose your temper.
- Get involved. Be a good family member and a committed employee. Do your fair share of the work at home and do not be a shirker at work.
- Be positive. Give genuine praise to work-mates and family members. Try not to get sucked into the moaning that goes on from time to time.
- Watch your language. Most swearing is not sinful but non-Christians tend to expect Christians to give it up; so do not deliberately confuse them!
- Be balanced. Religion should not be your only topic of conversation or church your only leisure activity. You need a good bit of 'secular' roughage in the diet for healthy living!
- Be normal! Jesus has not turned us into a combination of Mother Teresa and the Archangel Gabriel, so we do not need to put on spiritual 'airs and graces' or go around with holy smirks on our faces. Fanatics and frauds will put people off very quickly.

Be a friend
If you have not been a Christian very long you probably still have a lot of non-Christian friends and family members. These are precisely the people with whom you should be sharing your faith. Take time to keep these relationships strong. It would be wrong to neglect them anyway, and your friends will not be terribly impressed with your Christianity if you dump them because of it!

Go out of your way to cultivate other non-Christian friends. Play sport, take up a hobby or join the Rotary Club – avoid isolating yourself in a totally Christian world. Because of the pressure of time you will need to limit the number of jobs you do in the church if you are to develop friendships effectively.

Train

In one sense evangelism is the most natural thing in the world – just telling other people about something good that has happened to us. In practice, most of us would benefit from a little training. For example, could we explain the Christian message clearly in a few minutes? Can we say what God has done in our life without waffle, confusion or Christian clichés? What would we say in answer to the question, 'How can I become a Christian?' Sometimes your church fellowship will provide training to help tackle questions like these, or the leaders may be willing to contact an evangelistic agency to ask them to run a special training course for church members.

THE CHURCH AND EVANGELISM

If you find that you are specially gifted at evangelism, your church may want to make that your main function in the fellowship. Even if you do not feel gifted in this area, you can support the church's evangelistic programmes. Invite your friends to the special events, volunteer the use of your home for that coffee morning, distribute leaflets, do whatever you can to work with the church family in its evangelism.

You can probably help the church considerably, from your own experience, when it is planning a programme of evangelism. What would have attracted you to the church before you became a Christian? To what kind of evangelism would you have been open? What would have put you off? Some people in the church have been Christians for so long they have forgotten what it is like not to be one! Tell those responsible for evangelism some of your ideas. This will help them form a strategy for telling others of a similar age, or from a similar background, to yourself.

POWER AND EVANGELISM

God has changed our lives by his power. The same power is available to change others. You can have complete confidence in this. It may seem very hard to believe but your most obnoxious colleague at work or your most unpleasant relative can be made different by God's power. The same power which has been affecting people's lives down the centuries is just as potent today. God will be with us in power as we talk about what he has done for us. In fact he has given a promise to all those who take seriously the task of telling others: 'Go then, to all peoples everywhere and make them my disciples', said Jesus, 'And I will be with you always'!

9
Lifestyle

When we first become Christians, many of us make the mistake of thinking that God is only interested in the 'religious' part of our lives. We think he wants us to pray and go to church but we assume he has no interest in our normal day-to-day activities. Nothing could be further from the truth!

When we became Christians we became God's special children and, as our loving parent, God is vitally concerned about every aspect of our lives.

He has things to say about marriage, singleness, sex, money, work and leisure; you name it and he wants to help with it.

And he is uniquely qualified to do so: he made us, so he knows what makes us function properly. Remember those model aircraft kits you used to buy – a million small pieces of plastic and one microscopic tube of glue. They were hard enough to make *with* the instructions but without them we might as well have been looking for a needle in a haystack . . . wearing a blindfold! Our lives can *only* be lived properly if we follow the maker's instructions. As new Christians we are not always aware of what these instructions are, so we need help to discover them and to put them into practice.

Before we look at some of the principles, we need to be sure about one thing. Doing what God says in these areas is *not* what makes him love us; we cannot earn his love, recognition or approval. He gives us these as free gifts. We obey his rules, not as a way to earn spiritual Brownie points but because we love him and want to please him. When we try to obey God without love for him, we find we are performing a joyless, burdensome duty. This is both frustrating and discouraging as we realize we can never live up to his standards, no matter how hard we try. It is then only a short step to giving up completely on any attempt to do what God's standards demand. But if we love God we will *want* to do what he says. And, because we know that his love does not depend on how well we succeed, we can relax when we fail and be encouraged to try again.

THE PRINCIPLES

How do we know how God wants us to behave?

We will look at some specific issues in a moment but, whatever the issue, there are three principles which help us to discover how God wants us to live. They act as map, compass and guide in showing us the way forward. If the map shows that we should travel south, the compass registers 'S' and the guide assures us that we are heading southward, then we are probably on the right track.

The map

The Bible is the Christian's map. The first and most crucial step is to know what it says. It deals with some aspects of lifestyle clearly, but others are not addressed directly. For instance, we will not find references to luxury cruises, Porsches or abortion. What we will find, though, are principles relating to the use of time and money and to the value of life, along with some detailed application of those principles to situations that were faced by first-century Christians. Jesus' teaching and the letters in the New Testament set these out clearly.

The compass

When we have discovered what the Bible says on a subject relating to the way we live, we must adjust our behaviour to fit the Bible, not the other way round. We are the compass and need to decide how to bring ourselves into line with the map. This will mean thinking about how to apply the Bible's teaching in our own situation. As well as thinking carefully about it, we need to pray about it, asking God what he wants us to do. This is especially important where the Bible seems to be silent or unclear about an issue. One thing to remember here is that God will never guide us to do something which goes against what he has already said in the Bible.

The guide
When we have come to a decision about how to act in a particular situation, we need to check it out with a guide – someone who knows this territory pretty well. What do mature Christians say? Ask the leaders in your local church how they dealt with the issue in their own lives. How did they come to believe that was the right course of action? Do they think the decision you have come to is the right one? What advice would they give you?

Another way to find out what reliable Christians believe is to read a good book on the subject. Your

minister or the manager of your local Christian bookshop should be able to help you find one.

THE SPECIFICS

So much for general principles; now for some specifics. When we become Christians some of the ways we think and act need to change. We will look at two big issues in personal lifestyle and see how our new faith affects them.

Sometimes the Bible can be quite challenging...

Sex

The Bible's teaching on sex can come as a shock, especially if you have not had any real insight into Christianity before you became a Christian. Put plainly, this is it: sexual intercourse is great. In fact it was God's idea in the first place. Sex is never described as dirty or sinful in the Bible. But there are unmistakable rules about it. 'Sex is only to be expressed within marriage', and, 'homosexual activity is wrong' are two such rules.

This goes completely against society's current thinking. It could hardly be more directly opposed to behaviour in a society which preaches 'safe sex', encourages teenagers to go on the pill and whose 'heroes' in the media change partners with the same regularity as they change their cars. All this makes it pretty tough for a new Christian – hardly anyone seems to believe what the Bible says about sex any more. Well, take comfort from two things.

Firstly, remember William Penn's great saying,

Right is right, even if everyone is against it; and wrong is wrong, even if everyone is for it.

Something might be popular, but that does not mean it is right. Winston Churchill became pretty unpopular in 1938 when he told the country to prepare for war, but that did not stop him from being right! God's standards may be pretty unpopular in the 1990s but that says nothing about whether they are right or wrong.

Secondly, God's standards work! Casual, one-night-stand sex becomes deeply unfulfilling. Committed sex with a lifelong partner can be one of life's most rewarding experiences – a gourmet meal in comparison with the 'fast food' diet which illicit sex provides. It is also much healthier for individuals and society. The epidemics of VD and AIDS would be almost non-existent if God's 'chastity before marriage, faithfulness within marriage' standard was followed. The suggestion that condoms can prevent the spread of AIDS would be laughable were it not so pathetic. A much more effective solution is the radical, biblical alternative.

So much for the facts. Now you know them, what do you need to do? Unless we go on to change our behaviour, merely knowing about God's standards will not help us! As you change your lifestyle to one which pleases God more and more, it is helpful to remember some practical things:

• It will not be easy. Old habits die hard, so you may find yourself under great sexual temptation. Prepare for this in prayer and ask others to pray with you and for you. Avoid putting yourself in situations which encourage you to give in to the pressure. Plan how to fill your time with productive, alternative activity.

• Be bold. The longer you take to implement your new lifestyle the harder it is. Do not be conned into the 'I'll wait till I'm a little stronger in the faith' syndrome. That is about as logical as waiting until you feel a bit better before starting to take the medicine! Tough action, taken soon, will be a significant factor in your growth as a Christian.

• Be humble; that is, do not become a self-righteous prig! Just because *you* have decided to bring your sex life into line you should not look down your nose at others who have not. Your non-Christian friends will not take kindly to a holier-than-thou attitude.

• Be sensitive. Your boyfriend or girlfriend may not share your new faith. Explain carefully why you have decided to change your sexual behaviour. He or she may be hurt, thinking that you are rejecting him or her – or even that you have found someone else. Try to put yourself in their shoes and act accordingly.

● Be persistent. We live in a society which encourages promiscuity. Sex is used to sell everything from cars to cat food, and sexual indulgence is constantly encouraged. In this environment even having discovered God's standards you may slip back into sexual sin. God still loves you. Say sorry to him and pray for strength to remain pure. Be determined to live a life which pleases him. With his help, this is a battle you *can* win!

Money

This is probably the other main preoccupation of men and women at the end of the twentieth century. We cannot survive without it and the goods and services it buys. The problem is that it seems to dominate our thinking and can warp attitudes and change behaviour just as effectively as a drug. Just like a drug, the more we have of it the more we want, and each 'dose' has to be bigger than the last. All of us have felt the pressure of living in a world where 'the creed is greed and the god is gold'. So what is God's attitude?

Despite what many people think, the Bible does *not* say that money is the root of all evil. It is the *love* of money which is so corrupting (see 1 Timothy 6:10). When we love money it starts to own us rather than the other way round. These principles will help us make it our servant not our master:

● All our money is God's. When Jesus becomes our Lord he becomes the owner of every aspect of our lives, including our money. The right question to ask is not, 'How shall I spend my money?' But 'What would Jesus like me to do with *his* money?'

● Give generously. Some of God's money ought to be given for use in God's work. The Old Testament suggests that we should give ten per cent of our income to this. Ten per cent is still a useful guide-line today, but is a very difficult target for some to achieve. You may need to take a few months sorting out and rearranging your finances before you can get to this point. If you are more highly-paid you should find the ten per cent target easier to achieve and even to go beyond. Plan to give that money when you get your pay, rather than leaving it to see how much is left at the end!
● Avoid waste. Because our money is God's and can accomplish so much, we should try not to waste

it. Be careful about hasty purchases and impulse buying. It is not a bargain if you do not need it or if it is so cheap that it will break within days! Examine your motives. Are some brands bought for snob value? Are you buying to keep up with the neighbours or to impress the visitors? How much food gets thrown away?

● Plan borrowing carefully. Only use credit cards if you can be certain you will have the money to pay them off. Avoid debt like the plague. As far as possible, live within your means. Take time to consult someone with financial expertise – perhaps a friendly accountant in your church – before committing yourself to sizeable expenditure involving a long period of repayments. If you think you are already getting into financial difficulties tell someone *now*. The longer you leave it the harder it is to sort out.

● Warning! The map – or Bible – tells us that stealing is wrong. That includes trying to cheat the tax-man or submitting inflated expense claims. Watch out as well for the dangers of gambling. What starts out as an innocent flutter on the Derby can end in a full scale addiction.

Sex and money are not, of course, the only issues with which the Bible can help us. It is surprisingly full of God's views on almost all the issues which affect the way we live today. For example, he has things to say about alcohol abuse, marriage problems, divorce, bringing up children, work, leisure, old age and friendship. Find out what God thinks and begin to put it into practice.

10
Guidance

We can guide rockets to Mars, aeroplanes through
fog and deadly missiles to a small target hundreds
of miles away, but we seem incapable of providing a
'guidance system' to help the average human being!
Despite all the sophistication of the last part of the
twentieth century we are very unclear as to how we
should act for the best. We are still going round in
circles – only more quickly!

Each day thousands of people scan their
horoscope and some consult an astrologer. Many
more work themselves up into a lather of indecision
when trying to decide about their future. A book

entitled, *How to Make all the Right Decisions about your Future (in three easy steps)* would sell millions!

GUIDED, NOT PROGRAMMED

'Whom will I marry?' 'Shall I take this new job?' 'Should we move house?' 'Which church should I be part of?' 'Ought I to go to college?' 'What can I do to get out of this mess?' None of these questions has a slick, simple answer. Now that we have become Christians these concerns about our future boil down to one question, 'How can I discover what God wants me to do with my life?' As we look at some answers to this question, we should remember that we are sons and daughters of a wonderful heavenly Father. His desire is not to treat us like robots, programmed for every trivial task. We have genuine freedom. Some of us are far too intense about the issue of guidance, when God wants us to relax and to please ourselves. As long as we stay close to him we need not worry too much over most of our decisions. When we are walking close to him he can guide us, almost without our knowing!

There is one piece of really good news to start with: God wants to guide us! (Psalm 32:8.) It is his wish that in every way we become like Christ. He is not trying to hide anything from us or make things difficult. As a caring father he wants his children to have the best, so he can be approached for help with confidence!

In a world where people in general want to please themselves, we ought to make it clear that Christians want to please somebody else – God! There are two main reasons.

Firstly, he made us and therefore knows how we function best. Thousands of products carry this piece of advice, 'For best results, follow maker's instructions', and then give a list of recommendations. Stamped indelibly (and invisibly) on every human being are the same words! Christians look to God because he has the greatest knowledge about how we 'tick' as individuals.

Secondly, only God knows the future . . . so who better to help us prepare for it? When I was at college my sister sent me the words of an old song to encourage me. I have kept the letter in which she wrote them, and the words are:

'I know who holds the future,
And He'll guide me with his hand,
With God things don't just happen,
Everything by him is planned;
So as I face tomorrow
With its problems large and small,
I'll trust the God of miracles,
Give to Him my all.'

With this kind of God, no wonder we seek his help!

HOW DOES GOD GUIDE?

But how does God guide? What kinds of things does he use to help us? Here are eight aspects of his 'guidance system':

1 The Bible

Through regular reading of the Bible we come to see what kind of people God wants us to be. The Bible sets *general* boundaries around the areas we have to decide about. For instance, if you are a man seeking direction about getting married, the Bible will give advice about the qualities you should be looking for in a wife in terms of character. It will also indicate that she should be a Christian and that you should see a relationship with her as being permanent. The Bible will not give you her address and telephone number!

Sometimes a verse of the Bible leaps off the page at us and seems to indicate a specific course of action. This can be a real help . . . but be careful. Make sure God is giving the same message through some of his other methods of guidance as well.

2 Prayer

God can use our prayers to speak to us about his purpose for us, especially if we develop the art of listening! Over a period of time, as we listen to God, a sense of peace or 'rightness' can come over us about the decision we have to make. An inner conviction often develops that this course of action is the one we should take. The Bible puts it like this:

'Don't worry about anything, but in all your prayers ask God for what you need, always asking him with a thankful heart. And God's peace, which is far beyond human understanding will keep your hearts and minds safe in union with Christ Jesus.' (Philippians 4:6-7.)

3 Circumstances

God is often working for our good without us knowing it. Opportunities arise, coincidences occur and tragedy may strike. All these things form part of our lives. God can take all these events and use them to help us discern his will. The Old Testament tells the story of Esther, an ordinary 'commoner' who became queen. Her uncle helped her to see that she had not risen to prominence by chance; God could use that circumstance to enable Esther to rescue her people from death: 'Who knows,' her uncle said, 'maybe it was for a time like this that you were made queen!'

4 Common sense

The trouble with common sense is that it is not very common! God made us and he knows our gifts, skills and limitations. If you are five feet two inches tall he is probably not calling you to be a basketball player! If you are tone deaf you are unlikely to become a concert pianist. Occasionally, God overrules major obstacles like this but more often than not they are a pretty reliable guide to what our future is likely to be.

5 Leaders

The Bible puts us in a special relationship with the leaders in the church. 'Obey your leaders,' the New Testament tells us, ' . . . they keep watch over you . . .' Seek their advice. Ask for their help. Do not assume you can get by without consulting a mature Christian. At the very least they can listen carefully and pray sympathetically. At the best you could find yourself on the receiving end of some wise insights that had never occurred to you! Only pride prevents us getting someone else's input for our situation. Do not jeopardize your future by missing out on this vital method of guidance. The writer of the book of Proverbs put it like this,

> The way of the fool seems right to him, but a wise man listens to advice

6 The supernatural

God sometimes guides by speaking directly to us. An idea comes into our head right out of the blue; a mental picture fills our thoughts or words of instruction come into our mind. When people pray for us they may be given something from God to pass on to us. People have occasionally been given visions or God has used a dream to speak to them. Even angels get sent with messages from time to time.

Christians often seem to take one of two extreme positions about this form of guidance. Some will

not make any decision without some kind of special revelation from God; others think that this sort of guidance hardly every happens today. Be balanced! God can and does guide in these ways today. Be open to him doing so. However, do not be obsessed with this one method of guidance to the exclusion of others.

7 A sign

Sometimes people ask God to give them a sign to confirm what he wants. The classic example in the Bible is that of Gideon. One evening he put a fleece on the ground and asked God for it to be wet with dew and the ground dry when he got up the next morning, if God really wanted him to take a particular course of action. When God did this, Gideon asked him if he could do the trick the other way round for the next day! God did. After this convincing display Gideon was sure about what he had to do!

From time to time Christians have asked God to confirm his will by giving them a miraculous sign like this; many of them have been deeply disappointed! This form of guidance needs to be handled with real care. We cannot treat God as a kind of celestial magician, who can be asked to perform magic acts as a guarantee of his will. Taken to its logical conclusion this would remove the need for faith altogether. It has to be said that God does sometimes honour requests for this kind of sign but we need to be careful about putting God to the test. It is only likely to be a useful method of guidance on special occasions; we should not try it every time we want to discern God's will.

8 Duty

Not too popular, this, but very important. It is no good claiming that God wants you to phone up the boss to say you are sick so that you can take the day off to evangelize your friends! That is not what God wants; he sees that you have a duty to your employer. There is no need to pray about whether to pass on a bit of gossip you picked up at the women's meeting. Don't do it; you have a duty to others in the body of Christ. Some things are wrong and some are right. However much we pray for guidance in these matters, the facts will not change! Sometimes guidance is as simple as just doing what you know to be right.

Of course, not all these forms of guidance will be appropriate on each occasion. Usually we can act if a number of these things point in the same direction. When they seem to point in conflicting directions, wait . . . and keep on seeking. If all eight point clearly in the same direction God has got something pretty amazing up his sleeve for you!

THE PRINCIPLES

Now that we have established the methods God uses we can go on to look at the key principles by which we can discover his will in practice:

Ask

'Pretty obvious,' everybody thinks. But is it? How many times is God the *last* person we consult about a decision instead of the first? God does not ram his guidance down our throat, he waits to be asked.

That is why the Bible is constantly encouraging us to ASK. Jesus says, 'Ask and it will be given you.' James says, 'You do not get because you do not ask,' and Jesus reminds us that God delights to respond to 'those who ask him'! Let's remember to get God in on decision making early, before we have time to come to any conclusions which are hard to change.

Obedience

God will not guide us unless we are willing to do what he says. Too many people use God as one source of guidance among many. If they want to take his guidance they might, if it fits in with everything else. Or they treat God like a doctor who has diagnosed something they did not like the sound of . . . they go somewhere else for a second opinion. With God there is no second opinion! We must be ready to do what he says. We are soldiers standing before our commanding officer, not members of a debating society. Jesus himself was bound by this principle. Faced with the awesome prospect of the cross, he recoiled from its horrors. Despite this, he was clear about where his priority lay, 'Not what I want, but what you want,' he said to God. It is people with this attitude who are given God's guidance!

Action

Do not sit around in your Christian life waiting for some flash of lightning to guide you. Act on what is right and, as you do, be open to God speaking to you. Abraham was told by God to leave his home town, but not where to go! It was only as he *travelled* that God told him. It is much easier to steer a car that is moving, and it is much easier for God to guide us when we are in action for him.

11
Looking outwards

You will have heard of ingrowing toe-nails – a minor physical ailment; this chapter is about ingrowing eyeballs – a major spiritual ailment – and how to cure it! Most of this book has given the sort of help and advice that will help you get your life sorted out in a way that pleases God. It is all based on the understanding that, 'now I have made someone else the master of my life, I had better find out how he wants me to live and start to bring my life into line!'

We have looked at *my* prayer life, *my* future, *my* church, *my* spiritual gifts, etc, and it is all essential stuff. We must get these things right if we are to grow as Christians. But can you see how our eyeballs can get turned completely inwards? *My* this, *my* that . . . I have known Christians who assess every service, every ministry, every gift by what they can get out of it. We are in danger of breeding a self-centred, self-serving generation of Christians!

So, in addition to looking inward, we need to look outward in order to have a balanced Christian life. Jesus himself is our great example in this. He took time to meet own needs – food, sleep, relationship with his Father – but was still known supremely as 'the man for others'. He focused his life on God first, and then looked outward to the needy world. We fail to reproduce his attitude at our peril: God's order for true joy is still, **J**esus **O**thers, **Y**ourself!

Simply because we live in a society which is dominated by self interest, we are very vulnerable to 'ingrowing eyeballs'. The yuppie with his filofax and Porsche symbolizes much of the current self-seeking which is rapidly putting 'self' at the centre of our culture. Gordon Bailey summarizes our world in his poem, *The Whether Outlook*:

Whether I'm helpful when people despair;
Depends very largely on whether I care.
Whether I think that oppression's a crime,
Depends very largely on whether I've time.
Whether I go where my help is required,
Depends very largely on whether I'm tired.
Whether I'm generous, whether I'm mean,
Depends very largely on whether I'm keen;
Whether I honour the vows that I take,
Depends very largely on what I can make.
Whether I help someone burdened by care,
Depends very largely on whether I'm there.
Whether I love, or I hope, or I trust,
Depends very largely on whether I must.
Whether I comfort a friend who's afraid,
Depends very largely on whether I'm paid.
Whether I'll be just the same come next year,
Depends quite completely on whether I'm here!
(From *Plastic World*, STL.)

Take note. We are all infected. Religious selfishness is no answer to worldly selfishness – self*less*ness
is the answer. Ask God to help you to keep looking
out!

MISSION

Billions of people around the world still do not
know about Jesus. Millions do not have the freedom
to speak about him publicly for fear of arrest or
harassment. Hundreds of thousands do not have
any portion of the Bible in their own language.
Look over the walls of your own church, beyond
your own community, past the frontiers of your

own country and into this vastly needy world. We can take our faith so much for granted: we have a bewildering array of song books, cassettes, videos, books, magazines and ministries to help us in it. But this is in a world where whole tribes have never even seen a complete Bible, never mind owned one! In South America there are thirty ministers of the gospel for every million people; in India fifteen and in America over 1,400! What can we do to rectify this imbalance?

Pray

Find out about other countries. What are their specific needs and problems? What percentage of the population are Christians? Which agencies work there? Send away to some of these missionary societies for more information. Get a copy of *Operation World* (see p 128) which gives facts and figures about each country in the world, and use it to gather material for prayer. Adopt a missionary, perhaps with others in your house group, and commit yourself to regular prayer for them.

Give

It is said that American Christians spend more on pet food in fifty-two days than they give in a *year* to foreign mission! We are probably not much better. If your church supports mission, perhaps you could give an additional gift and earmark it for a named missionary or a specific project. Perhaps, over and above your regular giving, you could send a small, regular amount to some special overseas concern. Or what about a special parcel of 'goodies' to encourage a missionary? It is amazing how exciting it can be to receive packages from home. The parcel could contain anything from magazines to blankets! (You will need to check first with a missionary society that works in the area, in case there are local regulations to be aware of.)

Write

If you have never been alone in a strange county it is hard to imagine how welcome a letter can be. A letter to a missionary will give pleasure far beyond all the time and energy you put into writing it. Here are some clues to a good letter:

● Do not be 'over spiritual'. Write about local news items, sporting highlights or an occasional television programme. Give up-to-date information on 'births, deaths and marriages' in your church, if they are familiar with the church family. Let them know about the humorous incidents too.

● Write on special occasions. Remember to post in good time for anniversaries, birthdays and Christmas. Major occasions can highlight the loneliness when you are away from home.

● Include interesting newspaper or magazine cuttings, a photo of the kids, and the church magazine.

● Occasionally send a postcard, perhaps when you are on holiday. It will be encouraging for your missionary friends to be sent invitations to weddings too, even if you know they will not be able to come. At least they will feel less left out.

● Say you are praying for them (and do it!) and offer a verse from the Bible to encourage them.

● Do not expect a reply to every letter.

- You could experiment with putting a message on cassette or making an annual phone call.
- Be creative! Try to put yourself in their position and respond accordingly.

Go

Are you ready, if God calls, not only to look out but also to *go* out? God will be calling some of you reading this to work overseas. I pray that you will hear and respond to his call.

COMMUNITY

Nearer to home, but still largely ignored by many Christians, is the local community. As new Christians, the temptation is to dump all our old non-Christian friends, develop a new set of friendships and throw ourselves whole-heartedly into church life. This can lead to us ignoring the very people we are supposed to be reaching with the good news!

If we withdraw from all 'non-spiritual'

community activities the church becomes like a ghetto, increasingly absorbed in its own activities and progressively isolated from the community it is supposed to serve. The New Testament vision of the church – powerful, loving, relevant – is often replaced in twentieth-century Britain by a sterile, introverted, religious clique! Many people in your area probably do not even know where your church meets, never mind what it teaches or who its leaders are. Christians must start looking out beyond their local church organizations . . . and now is a good time to start!

So what can an ordinary Christian with a bit of initiative do to make sure that he or she does not get detatched from 'community' life? There are three basic steps:

1 Re-discover your neighbourhood
Do something you may never have done before: walk along the streets and take a good look round! What are the strengths and weaknesses of the area? What kind of people live behind those net curtains? How would Jesus have responded to what you see as you go on your walkabout? Find out all you can about the area – the library and local government office are good places to start. A local social worker, doctor or policeman would also be good points of reference; each is likely to have clear insights into the specific needs in your community.

2 Re-order your priorities
Simple to say; tough to do! You need to ensure that time is given to activities outside your own fellowship. Perhaps you could even manage one

night a week in a 'non-churchy' pursuit. You will
have to make this a priority if it is going to work.
It is often easier if your partner or children are
included – then family time is also expanded. It
may mean having to turn down another job you are
asked to do at church to preserve this 'community'
time.

3 Re-evaluate your programme
Just because the church has a football team you do
not have to join it! You could join another local
club. If you like stamp collecting (or photography
or knitting or mud-wrestling!) think twice before
starting a group at the church. Why not join one
already in existence locally? Support the school
band, go to the local fête, join the operatic society,
sign up for the darts team.

There are many opportunities in our own
localities to exercise a major influence for good.
School governing bodies need the involvement of
parents and additional representation from others
in the community. Trade unions need shop stew-
ards and other officers. Residents' associations need
secretaries. Meals-on-wheels need volunteers.

Do not forget the influence of the media. Is your
local rag looking for a volunteer news reporter?
What about the local radio station – do they want
help in any area? Is there a local hospital that could
do with help on its 'in-house' radio station?

The things on these lists give a taste of the possibilities; they represent a small fraction of the opportunities we have to serve our community.

ISSUES

Very big issues confront us today as never before. Most of the problems have been around for a long time but television brings them into our homes with a sharpness and an authority which is hard to avoid. Racism in South Africa, persecution behind the Iron Curtain, AIDS, sexual-abuse, alcoholism, abortion, surrogate-motherhood and unemployment have all featured on the news headlines during the past year. They affect us all – Christians and non-Christians alike – and are part of the outworking of sin in our world.

As new Christians it would be wrong to bury our heads, ostrich-like, in the sand and hope these problems go away. And we cannot indulge in the luxury of the 'I'm all right, Jack' version of Christianity which is content to let the world go to hell while we enjoy the benefits of our personal salvation. These issues bother God and, if they bother him, they ought to bother us! But what can we do?

Avoid despair
Do not let the size of the problems put you off. We can be threatened into inactivity and disillusionment by the sheer enormity of all that is wrong with the world. Remember that Everest and your stairs are climbed in precisely the same way – one step at a time!

Act!
Are you concerned about the low levels of overseas aid? Write to the Prime Minister. Violence on television? Contact the relevant broadcasting authority. The presence of a sex shop? Talk to your local councillor.

Give money, sign petitions, write letters and enthuse others. Each act, however small, combines with the efforts of other people to have a potentially major impact. The policies of government, the attitudes of broadcasters and the behaviour of large multi-national companies have been changed by persistent, polite protest; often by just a handful of people!

Remember your Christian heritage

Major changes in society have been brought about by Christians in the past. For example, slavery was abolished by Act of Parliament in 1833 as the result of the struggles of a group of Christians over a number of years. William Wilberforce, their chief spokesmen, died only months after the Act became law, much of his life having been dedicated as a Christian to fighting the slave trade. And there are dozens of other examples of Christians making a difference in the world – hospitals established, orphanages founded, laws passed, customs changed and charitable associations started.

You may only recently have become a Christian but you now stand in a long tradition of 'change-agents'. *You* with your church family . . . *you* can make a difference. Go for it!

12
And finally...

By this stage in the book you probably feel you are getting to grips with the basic ingredients of Christian living. If you have read the chapters carefully you will have gained enough information to lay firm foundations for the future. But you have not built the building yet! The construction work will take the rest of your life.

BUILDING ON THE FOUNDATIONS

The following suggestions will help as you begin to apply this material day by day and as you plan for your future as one of God's family.

Go for steady progress!
This book gives lots of ideas to think about and plenty of things to be doing in order to grow as a Christian. You could be excused for thinking that

you need thirty hours in a day, with a ten-day week to fit it all in! Relax! Take it a bit at a time. Steady progress is better, in the long-run, than three months of frantic activity followed by a state of nervous exhaustion. It is not a sin to have a hobby, play sport or go to the pictures. God is with us in our leisure and can use us just as effectively there as in our 'churchy' activities.

Try not to get too intense about the Christian life. Develop a good sense of humour and do not take yourself too seriously. Laugh regularly with (but never at!) other people. Believe me, *God* often finds us amusing so the sooner we get in on the joke and learn to laugh at ourselves the better! This ability to laugh at ourselves is a key factor in moving towards maturity. It can protect us from pride, deliver us from depression, keep us from criticism and save us from stress. As a general rule, most Christians should take God more seriously and themselves less seriously.

Keep going!
The Devil uses a variety of things to get people to give up their Christian faith: pressure from friends or family, failure, a crisis, other attractions or some sin we refuse to put right. It could even be something trival like the minister forgetting to visit you in hospital or not being asked to sing in the choir or not getting chosen as a house group leader.

He will use any ploy to try to separate you from God and his people. Be aware of this, and do not let anything knock you off course in your faith. Determine right now, with God's help, to let nothing get between you and God or between you and his people. You are in a committed relationship with God, one even more permanent than the marriage bond which was promised to be 'till death us do part'. In our relationship with God, even death does not bring separation, only more joy!

Do not be discouraged!
You may feel fed up with how slow your progress seems to be in the Christian life. You could easily become disillusioned if none of your friends and family show any interest in Jesus. It can be pretty discouraging if your church seems stuck in a rut or the house group is as enthusiastic as a turkey at Christmas.

But do not let discouragement rob you of joy, stop you witnessing, make you less committed to the church or push you into reverse in your spiritual growth. Many of the great achievements in God's kingdom took years to accomplish, triumphing over incredible odds and only finally succeeding after countless setbacks and disappointments. William Carey had to work for seven years in India before a single person was converted; missionaries in New Zealand had to wait nine years and in Tahiti, sixteen!

Keep on keeping on. Persistence is crucial. God will honour your faithfulness and you will have the joy of his 'well done' on your life. You may also find yourself accomplishing something very significant for God!

STILL A LOT MORE TO COME

You have reached Watford on your trip from London to Glasgow; you are just out of Dover harbour on a voyage to France; you are just out of nappies on your journey to adulthood: in other words, just getting started! When Winston Churchill was asked if the war was at an end in 1942, he said, 'This is not the end, it is not even the beginning of the end, but it is perhaps the end of the beginning.' That is where we have arrived, 'the end of the beginning'.

As growing Christians we have a great deal still to discover.

More about the Bible

There is the Bible's teaching to discover, and all the characters in it to find out about. There are tough subjects which are hard to understand, such as the second coming of Jesus, the Trinity, heaven and hell. There are subjects which are easy to understand but hard to put into practice, such as love, joy, peace and patience! Discover what the book of Job teaches about suffering; learn from Solomon about wisdom, from Daniel about boldness, from Ruth about faithfulness, from Jesus about overcoming temptation and from Joseph about defeating sexual sin.

More about the church

What can churches other than my own teach me about living the Christian life? How can I benefit from the insights which Christians on other continents have about being a Christian today? What lessons can be learnt from Christians in other centuries – how did they handle difficult issues like persecution and compromise? There are many things to be learnt from missionaries like Gladys Aylward, pioneers like William Booth, church planters like John Wesley and preachers like George Whitefield.

More about ourselves

You are probably just beginning to see yourself as God sees you. The more you understand your strengths and weaknesses the better your spiritual progress will be. But we are a complex mixture of our parents and the factors which influenced our childhood and youth; a potpourri of emotions, attitudes, habits and actions. As God gently allows us to see ourselves for what we really are, he begins the process of changing us to be like Jesus. And there is a lot of work to do!

More about God
This is the most important area of discovery possible. There will always be more of God to find out about and experience. More about his character, more about his dealings with nations and individuals, more about his power. Let me urge you to return to God again and again, asking not merely for more strength or more knowledge but for more of him! Come, Oliver-like, to the God above all gods, the Lord above all lords, saying, 'Please, Father, is there any more?' There always is!

OTHER BOOKS AND FURTHER INFORMATION

To help understand the Bible

● *General*
The Lion Handbook To The Bible, eds D and P Alexander. Lion Publishing.
The New Bible Dictionary, ed J Douglas. IVP.

● *Commentaries*
The New Bible Commentary Revised, ed D Guthrie. IVP. This is a one-volume commentary on the whole Bible.
Bible Study Commentary Series, various authors. Scripture Union. One commentary generally covers one book of the Bible. The commentaries are designed to be read on a daily basis alongside a passage of the Bible, and are broken up into daily sections.
Tyndale Bible Commentaries, various authors. IVP. These help with more detailed Bible study. Most deal with one book only.

● *Bible reading notes*
Alive to God, Daily Bread, Daily Notes. These are all published by Scripture Union and provide the framework for a daily time of Bible reading and prayer. Each is designed for use over three months and is dated accordingly. *Keep Growing with God* is an undated booklet which, over the course of ten days, gives you a sample of each approach.

Every Day With Jesus is published by Crusade for World Revival and offers an alternative approach to a daily time alone with God.

● *Bible study*
Get More From Your Bible, B Abshire. Scripture Union.
Bible Study That Works, D Thompson. Scripture Union.
These two books are for people who want to discover how to read and understand the Bible for themselves. *Bible Study That Works* looks at the basic principles of understanding the Bible. *Get More From Your Bible* takes these a little further and demonstrates five basic methods of Bible study.

Answers to questions about Christian faith
The Case For Christianity, C Chapman. Lion Publishing.
It Makes Sense, S Gaukroger. Scripture Union. There is also a Study Edition available, designed for use by small groups, published by Scripture Union.

Books explaining the Christian faith
This Is Christianity, P Cotterell. IVP.
Know The Truth: Handbook of Christian Belief, B Milne. IVP.

Information for prayer
Operation World: Handbook for World Intercession, P Johnstone. Send The Light.